DBT Made Easy: A Comprehensive Guide to Balancing Opposing Ideas and Finding Your Inner Peace.

Maryellen J. Bond

Introduction

Discover the Power of DBT:

As a therapist who has seen the transformative power of Dialectical Behavior Therapy (DBT), I am excited to give this comprehensive guide to help you understand and apply this evidence-based therapy in your own life.

DBT was developed by Dr. Marsha Linehan in the late 1980s with the goal of providing an effective treatment for persons suffering from borderline personality disorder (BPD). It has now been discovered, however, to be effective for persons suffering from a wide range of mental health concerns, including depression, anxiety, substance use disorders, and eating disorders.

One of DBT's unique features is its emphasis on reconciling opposing points of view or dialectics. Individuals, for example, may struggle with the acceptance and change dialectic, in which they desire to accept themselves as they are while also making positive changes in their lives. DBT teaches people how to deal with opposing ideas by using techniques including mindfulness, emotion control, distress tolerance, and interpersonal effectiveness.

In research, DBT has been shown to be a successful treatment for persons with BPD, reducing symptoms such as self-harm, suicide behavior, and sorrow. However, it has been discovered to be beneficial for people suffering from a variety of mental health disorders. DBT was found to be effective in reducing feelings of despair and anxiety in patients with mood disorders, according to a study published in the Journal of Affective Disorders.

Another study published in the Journal of Consulting and Clinical Psychology revealed that DBT was effective in reducing opioid addiction in people who had previously used the drug. These findings highlight DBT's versatility as a treatment option for a wide range of mental health conditions.

This book will examine DBT in full, covering its history, theoretical foundations, and practical applications. It will include exercises and activities to help you build and use your skills in mindfulness, emotion management, distress tolerance, and interpersonal effectiveness.

One of the book's goals is to make DBT available to everyone, not just therapists. DBT skills can help you not only deal with mental health issues, but also improve your overall well-being and relationships.

I have firsthand experience with DBT's transformational power, and I am glad to share it with you. This book will assist you whether you are coping with mental health challenges or simply wish to improve your quality of life.

It is my hope that this book may inspire you to look into the possibilities of DBT and see the potential for personal growth and change. Let us go together down the path to a more fulfilling and balanced living.

Chapter 1

Ways for awareness: Staying Present and Engaged in the Present.

In this chapter, we will look at the conception of awareness and how it may be used as a strong tool in Dialectical Behavior Therapy(DBT).

Awareness is the practice of being completely present and engaged in the moment, without judgement or distraction. It's a core skill in DBT and has been shown to be effective in reducing symptoms of anxiety, depression, and emotional dysregulation.   One of the most significant benefits of awareness is its capability to help people in regulating their feelings.

Awareness, according to exploration, can help reduce emotional reactivity and increase emotional regulation. This implies that people who exercise awareness are better at managing their feelings when effects are delicate or stressful.

In addition to emotion operation, Awareness can help with anxiety and depression symptoms. According to a study published in the Journal of Psychiatric Research, awareness- grounded curatives were effective in reducing anxiety and depression symptoms in cases of people who had suffered trauma. Another study published in the Journal of Alternative and reciprocal drugs revealed that awareness contemplation helped habitual pain victims reduce their melancholy and anxiety symptoms.

One of the most common awareness practices used in DBT is the practice of Awareness

Contemplation. Sitting still and fastening on the breath without judgement, covering studies and passions as they arise, and gently directing the attention back to the breath, is what awareness contemplation includes. This approach helps people gain mindfulness of their studies and feelings, as well as the capability to observe them without getting caught up in them. Other awareness ways include aware dining, aware walking, and aware body reviews. Paying attention to the taste, smell, and texture of food, as well as hunger and wholeness sensations, is what aware eating includes. Being completely present and engaged in the act of walking, passing passions in the bases and legs as well as the surroundings, is what aware walking includes. aware body reviews involve precisely fastening on different sections of the body, noting passions, and relaxing. One of the most significant benefits of Awareness is its capability to help people in developing a nonjudgmental station toward themselves and others. This station of acceptance and compassion can be especially good for persons who struggle with tone- review, demotion, or guilt. Learning to observe studies and feelings without judgement might help people produce a more sympathetic and tolerant station toward themselves and others.

To epitomise, awareness is an important skill that may be employed to enhance emotional control, reduce anxiety and depression symptoms, and cultivate a nonjudgmental station toward oneself and others. By incorporating awareness into their diurnal lives, people can learn to be entirely present and absorbed in the moment, performing in a deeper sense of serenity and good. We'll look at emotion regulation in the following chapter and how it can be used to ameliorate internal health and well- being.

Chapter 2

Emotion Regulation Skills: Techniques for Dealing with Strong Emotions.

Emotions are a natural and vital part of the human experience. They have an impact on our judgments, motivate our behaviours, and provide us with a rich inner world of experience. Emotions, on the other hand, might become overwhelming, powerful, or difficult to manage at times. Having tools and tactics to regulate our emotions and find a sense of balance can be useful in these situations.

Dialectical Behavior Therapy (DBT) combines mindfulness, cognitive-behavioural, and interpersonal techniques to offer a variety of evidence-based emotion control treatments. In this chapter, we will look at some of the key emotion regulation abilities in DBT, such as detecting and categorising feelings, enhancing positive emotions, reducing negative emotions, and dealing with crises.

Emotion Recognition and Labelling
The first step toward emotional control is becoming aware of our feelings. We are frequently so engrossed in our emotions that we are unconscious of how we are feeling. DBT begins with developing the ability to be mindful, which requires paying attention to the present moment with nonjudgmental awareness.

Mindfulness can assist us in recognizing and examining our feelings without becoming overwhelmed or reacting. Once we've identified our emotions, we can associate them with specific phrases. This can help us better understand and communicate our emotional experiences, as well as reduce their severity.

Increasing Positive Emotions

Another key method for controlling emotions is to increase happy sentiments. Positive emotions can shield us from negative emotions while also delivering a sense of well-being and enjoyment. DBT uses a variety of techniques to increase positive emotions, including practising gratitude, engaging in pleasurable activities, and establishing mastery.

The practice of giving thanks requires intentionally focusing on and expressing gratitude for the excellent aspects of our existence. This can be performed through journaling, sharing with others, or simply sitting in silence. Selecting activities that bring us joy or pleasure and making time to do them on a regular basis is engaging in pleasant activities. Setting goals and working toward them can provide a sense of satisfaction and pride while also fostering mastery.

Negative Emotions Reduction

Of course, negative emotions are an unavoidable part of life. However, rather than completely eliminating negative emotions, DBT focuses on reducing their intensity and duration. One method for minimising negative feelings is to engage in opposing activities.

When we are in a foul mood, we should deliberately do the opposite of what we want to do. If we are sad and wish to isolate ourselves, we may instead reach out to a friend or loved one. This can help us modify our emotional experience and[1] lessen the severity of our unpleasant emotions.

Taking Care of Emergencies

Finally, DBT offers crisis management methods, which can be effective when emotions become unusually powerful or overwhelming. These

---

[1]

abilities include self-soothing, diversion, and radical acceptance.

Self-soothing includes acts that are both comfortable and calming, such as taking a warm bath or practising deep breathing. Distraction is the intentional shifting of our attention away from the overwhelming feeling and toward a task or activity that takes our whole attention. Radical acceptance includes accepting the situation or sensation as it is, without judgement or resistance.

Finally, emotional regulation skills are essential for dealing with overpowering emotions and achieving a sense of equilibrium in our lives. DBT provides evidence-based emotion regulation strategies such as emotion detection and categorization, strengthening positive emotions, lowering negative emotions, and managing crises. By honing these skills, we can learn to navigate our emotions with greater ease and resilience.

Chapter 3

Coping Techniques for Difficult Situations: Distress Tolerance

Life may be stressful, and we all have to deal with challenging situations. These stressful situations, whether they be a breakup, a job loss, or financial difficulties, can leave us feeling overwhelmed and concerned about the future. In these instances, having coping strategies that allow us to absorb the pain while moving on is crucial.

Dialectical Behaviour Therapy (DBT) teaches distress tolerance skills that can be used in difficult situations. These abilities are intended to help people cope with painful emotions and situations without engaging in destructive behaviour.

Studies have shown that distress tolerance skills can help reduce feelings of depression, anxiety, and other mental health issues. A study published in the Journal of Psychiatric Research, for example, revealed that using distress tolerance skills was associated with lower levels of depressive symptoms in people suffering from major depression.

Acceptance is an important aspect of distress tolerance. Acceptance includes acknowledging and recognizing difficult emotions and experiences rather than ignoring or avoiding them. This does not entail giving up or succumbing to the situation, but rather admitting its existence and the possibility of responding in a healthy and adaptive manner.

Another important aspect of distress tolerance is **Distraction**. Participating in activities that divert our attention away from the painful incident or feeling is classified as distraction. Distraction tactics include watching a movie, taking a walk, or engaging in a pastime.

Self-calming is another useful skill for coping with stress. This means learning how to soothe and care for oneself in stressful times. Self-calming pastimes include taking a warm bath, drinking a cup of tea, and listening to soothing music.

Tolerating distress necessitates **Extreme Acceptance** as well. Accepting reality without judgement or resistance is what radical acceptance means. This can be challenging, especially when the outcome is not what we expected or anticipated. However, practising radical acceptance can help us let go of feelings of rage, frustration, and disappointment and move forward in a more positive direction.

Finally, **Mindfulness** is an important stress-reduction technique. Being mindful requires being in the present moment and aware of it without judgement or attachment. Mindfulness meditation can help people stay grounded in difficult situations and reduce the intensity of unpleasant feelings.

It is crucial to recognize that distress tolerance is not a one-size-fits-all solution. Different abilities may be better suited to different people and situations. It is critical to consult with a therapist or mental health professional to determine which skills will be most beneficial to you.

Distress tolerance is a useful technique for dealing with difficult situations and emotions. DBT provides a variety of coping skills that can assist people in dealing with tough emotions and situations without engaging in harmful behaviours. Studies have shown that distress tolerance skills can help reduce feelings of depression, anxiety, and other mental health issues. Acceptance, diversion, self-soothing, radical acceptance, and mindfulness can help people cope with difficult experiences in a healthy and adaptive way.

Chapter 4

Interpersonal effectiveness skills: Techniques for Improving Communication and Relationships

As human beings, our lives are shaped by the relationships we have with others. These relationships can bring us great joy and fulfilment, but they can also be a source of stress, conflict, and pain. Developing strong interpersonal effectiveness skills is essential for improving communication and relationships, both personally and professionally.

Interpersonal effectiveness skills are a key component of Dialectical Behavior Therapy (DBT). DBT teaches individuals how to navigate challenging interpersonal situations, improve communication skills, and build healthy relationships. The four main skills of interpersonal effectiveness are: Objective Effectiveness, Relationship Effectiveness, Self-respect Effectiveness, and Mindfulness Effectiveness.

Objective Effectiveness involves understanding and communicating our needs and wants in a clear and direct manner. It involves identifying our goals and priorities, and communicating them in a way that is respectful and assertive. Research has shown that individuals who are able to effectively communicate their needs and wants are more likely to have satisfying and fulfilling relationships.

Relationship Effectiveness involves considering the needs and wants of others in our interactions with them. It involves balancing our own needs with the needs of others, and being able to communicate in a way that is respectful and empathetic. Research has shown that individuals who are able to demonstrate empathy and consideration towards others are more likely to have positive and lasting relationships.

Self-respect Effectiveness involves maintaining our sense of self-worth and boundaries in our interactions with others. It involves being able to say no when necessary, and setting healthy boundaries to protect our physical and emotional well-being. Research has shown that individuals who are able to set and maintain healthy boundaries are more likely to have positive self-esteem and overall life satisfaction.

Mindfulness Effectiveness involves being present and non-judgmental in our interactions with others. It involves being able to recognize and manage our own emotional reactions, and to approach interactions with a calm and open mindset. Research has shown that individuals who are able to approach interactions with mindfulness and emotional regulation are more likely to have positive outcomes and less conflict.

Developing these interpersonal effectiveness skills takes time and practice. Some techniques that can help include:

- **Active listening**: actively listening to what others are saying and responding in a way that shows you have understood their message.
- **Using "I" Statements**: using statements that express your own thoughts and feelings, rather than blaming or accusing others.
- **Validation**: acknowledging and validating the feelings of others, even if you do not agree with their perspective.
- **Role-playing**: practising interpersonal skills in a safe and controlled environment, such as with a therapist or trusted friend.

Developing interpersonal effectiveness skills is essential for building strong and healthy relationships, both personally and professionally. By learning and practising these skills, individuals can improve their communication, manage conflict more effectively, and create more fulfilling relationships. DBT offers a comprehensive approach to developing these skills, and can be an effective treatment for individuals struggling with interpersonal challenges.

Chapter 5

Mindfulness at its core: Developing mindfulness and acceptance of one's own thoughts and feelings.

Mindfulness is a fundamental skill in Dialectical Behavior Therapy (DBT) that is essential for emotional regulation and overall well-being. Mindfulness entails paying attention to the current moment with curiosity and non-judgment. Core mindfulness, in particular, is a skill that involves developing awareness and acceptance of one's own thoughts and feelings.

The goal of core mindfulness is to notice and explain our experiences without criticising them. When presented with strong emotions or difficult situations, we may react rashly or attempt to avoid our feelings totally. By practising core mindfulness, we can learn to approach our experiences with inquiry and openness rather than judgement or avoidance.

There are numerous key components of core mindfulness that may help us develop awareness and acceptance of our thoughts and feelings. Here are a few examples:

1. To observe means to pay attention to our experiences without striving to change them. We can observe our ideas, feelings, and body experiences without judging or criticising them. For example, if we recognize that we are experiencing anxiety, we can examine our

thoughts and physical sensations without seeking to push or control the anxiety.

2. Describing requires us to verbalise our experiences without adding judgement or interpretation. We can express ourselves without attaching labels or judgments to our thoughts, feelings, and experiences. When we are unhappy, we might express physical sensations in our body, such as chest heaviness or a lump in our throat.

3. Participating is being completely present in the situation and not trying to change or deny our feelings. We can engage in our experiences if we are open and curious. If we are anxious in a social situation, for example, we can engage in it rather than avoid or try to escape it.

4. A nonjudgmental attitude is one in which we approach our experiences with curiosity and openness rather than judgement or evaluation. We can be aware of our feelings and thoughts without labelling them as good or bad, right or

wrong. This allows us to be more accepting and sympathetic to ourselves and our circumstances.

By practising core mindfulness, we can cultivate a more balanced and accepting attitude toward our thoughts and feelings. This can help us manage difficult emotions, improve our relationships, and improve our overall well-being. Mindfulness is a powerful skill that may be used in a variety of settings, including therapy, self-help, and daily life.

To recap, core mindfulness is a DBT practice that comprises increasing awareness and acceptance of our thoughts and feelings. We can practise observing, describing, participating, and assuming a nonjudgmental position to develop a more balanced and tolerant response to our experiences. Mindfulness is a great approach for dealing with difficult emotions, strengthening relationships, and overall well-being.

Chapter 6

Finding a Happy Medium Between Rational and Emotional Thinking

As humans, we are multidimensional individuals possessing intellectual and emotional sides to our thinking. We frequently struggle to balance these two sides of ourselves, which makes decision-making and emotion control difficult. DBT advocates the notion of Wise Mind, which is the integration of cognitive and emotional thinking that results in a balanced perspective and decision-making process. This chapter examines how to reach our Wise Mind as well as the research that supports its utility in reducing symptoms of various mental health issues.

According to study, persons who suffer from depression have a proclivity for negative thinking, which leads to a lack of motivation and thoughts of hopelessness. According to a study published in the Journal of Consulting and Clinical Psychology, teaching persons suffering from depression how to use their Wise Mind resulted in a reduction in symptoms and an improvement in overall mood.

So, how can we make our Mind Wise? Mindfulness practice is one technique. Mindfulness is being conscious or alert to something without being judgemental. It allows us to explore our thoughts and feelings without becoming caught up in them. By practising mindfulness, we can learn to recognize when our emotions take over and return to a rational perspective.

Emotional regulation is another important aspect of accessing our Wise Mind. It requires properly detecting and managing our emotions. Such activities include deep breathing, increasing muscular relaxation, and writing. By managing our emotions, we can prevent them from taking over and clouding our rational thinking.

Along with mindfulness and emotion management, interpersonal effectiveness is an important component in accessing our Wise Mind. Interpersonal effectiveness requires effectively communicating our demands and limitations to others. By doing so, we can prevent our emotions from interfering with good conversation and decision-making.

It is vital to acknowledge that attaining our Wise Mind is not an easy task. It takes time and effort to learn to balance our intellectual and emotional thinking. The advantages, on the other hand, are well worth the effort. By accessing our Wise Mind, we may make more informed decisions, better control our emotions, and improve our overall well-being.

To recap, maintaining a healthy balance of rational and emotional thinking is essential for our mental health and well-being. By accessing our Wise Mind through mindfulness, emotion regulation, and interpersonal effectiveness, we can learn to balance these two aspects of ourselves and make better informed decisions. Let us continue to develop our Minds so that we can live a more fulfilling and balanced life.

Chapter 7

Dialectical Thinking: Conflict Resolution and Finding Middle Grounds

As a therapist, I frequently see clients who struggle to make decisions, especially when challenged with opposing thoughts and feelings. Dialectical Thinking, a fundamental principle of Dialectical Behavior Therapy (DBT), offers a powerful technique for resolving such disagreements and finding a common ground.

At its core, dialectical thinking is a technique for comprehending how two seemingly opposing or conflicting ideas can both be true at the same time. Dialectical thinking encourages us to see the nuances and shades of grey in complex situations rather than seeing them in black and white.

According to research, the ability to engage in dialectical thinking is associated with improved emotional control and resilience, problem-solving abilities, and interpersonal interactions. In reality, according to a study published in the Journal of Personality and Social Psychology, those who were taught to think dialectically were more fitted to deal with interpersonal conflicts and handle complex problems.

DBT typically uses dialectical thinking to aid clients in resolving conflicts within themselves, between themselves and others, and between their own needs and the needs of others. When clients embrace both sides of a problem and find a middle ground, they are more equipped to make long-term decisions that are profitable and sustainable.

The "Dialectical Synthesis" is one of the most important abilities required for dialectical reasoning. This skill requires identifying two competing ideas and determining how to merge them into a coherent and meaningful whole. This approach requires a willingness to accept the inherent contradictions and paradoxes of intricate conditions, as well as an openness to new and imaginative solutions.

Another important aspect of dialectical thinking is the ability to validate all sides of a conflict. Validating someone's viewpoint may not always require agreeing with them, but rather recognizing that their viewpoint is understandable and valuable. When both sides of a problem are validated, individuals are better able to build trust and understanding with others and work toward more mutually beneficial solutions.

DBT commonly employs dialectical thinking in conjunction with other skills such as mindfulness and emotional regulation to help clients achieve a greater sense of balance and well-being. Clients are better equipped to deal with life's challenges and build deeper, more rewarding relationships if they accept the complexities of their thoughts and emotions and learn to synthesise seemingly contradictory ideas into a logical whole.

Overall, dialectical thinking is a powerful and revolutionary way for resolving disputes and finding common ground. Accepting life's paradoxes and complexity and learning to validate both sides of a conflict can help people develop a deeper sense of calm, understanding, and resilience.

Chapter 8

Self-validation: Accepting and Recognizing your Own Emotions and Experiences.

As a therapist, one of the most important tools I employ to help my clients is the concept of self-validation. The act of acknowledging and accepting one's own emotions and experiences without seeking external approval is known as self-validation. In this chapter, we'll define self-validation, why it's important, and how you may use it in your own life.

What is the definition of self-validation?
Self-validation is the process of acknowledging and accepting one's own emotions and experiences. It is the act of acknowledging and affirming one's own emotions, thoughts, and experiences without seeking approval from others. When we give ourselves permission to feel the way we do and recognize the reality of our own experiences, we practise self-validation.

What is the significance of self-esteem?
Self-validation is essential because it helps us form a positive relationship with ourselves. When we learn to validate our own emotions and experiences, we become more self-aware and tolerant of ourselves. We develop emotional resilience, which allows us to cope better with stress and difficult situations. We also become

less reliant on external validation, which may be both empowering and liberating.

Self-validation is a key part of emotional well-being, according to study. Self-validation practitioners, according to study, are less likely to suffer from anxiety, depression, and other mental health disorders. They are also more likely to have healthier connections and be content with their lives.

How to Carry Out Self-Validation

Self-validation may appear difficult at first, especially if you are used to seeking acceptance from others. With time and work, it may, nevertheless, become a natural part of your daily routine. Here are some pointers to help you practise self-validation:

1. Recognize Your sentiments: The first stage in self-validation is to recognize your sentiments. Take a breather to check in with yourself. What are your current emotions like? Recognize and name your emotions.

2. Accept Your Emotions: Once you've acknowledged your emotions, accept them without judgement. Remember that all feelings are legitimate and natural. It is acceptable to feel sorrow, rage, or fright.

3. Validate Your Experience: Validate your experience by stating that you have true and valid feelings. Remind yourself that you are natural and there's nothing abnormal about feeling the way you feel.

4. Practice Self-Compassion: Be kind and sympathetic to yourself. Remember that everyone makes errors and experiences difficult emotions. Treat yourself with the same care and concern that you would show a friend.

5. Take Care of Yourself: Take care of yourself by doing things that make you joyful. This could include engaging in physical activity, practising mindfulness, or spending time with family and friends.

6. Seek Assistance: If you're having difficulty validating your own emotions, don't be afraid to seek assistance from a therapist or a trusted friend. They can help you overcome whatever problems you may be facing.

Self-validation is an important aspect of emotional well-being. It means acknowledging and embracing your own emotions and experiences without seeking validation from others. When we practise self-validation, we gain emotional resilience and become less reliant on external approval from others. With time and effort, self-validation can become a natural part of our daily routine, supporting us in creating a good connection with ourselves and increasing our overall well-being.

Chapter 9

Building Positive Experiences: Strategies for Creating a More Fulfilling Life

As a therapist, I have surely worked with many people who had sad thoughts and feelings. It is, nevertheless, feasible to generate more enjoyable experiences and a more fulfilling life. In this chapter, I'll discuss techniques for producing positive experiences as well as Dialectical Behavior Therapy (DBT), which can help people overcome negative thoughts and feelings.

One of the most effective strategies to create positive experiences is to concentrate on the current moment. When we focus on the present, we can fully engage with our surroundings and experiences, which leads to a more cheerful outlook on life. The practice of mindfulness, or being fully present in the moment, is an effective way to develop this skill. Mindfulness can be practised by setting aside a few minutes each day to sit quietly, focus on their breath, and observe their thoughts and feelings without judgement.

Cultivating positive relationships with people is another method for creating pleasurable experiences. It has been shown that having strong social support networks increases happiness and improves overall health. If you want to build healthy relationships, surround yourself with individuals that lift you up and inspire you. Spend time with people who share your interests and values, and volunteer or do acts of kindness in your community.

Practising appreciation is another effective way to increase joyful experiences. When we focus on what we are grateful for, we tend to experience more joy and contentment in our lives. To practise thankfulness, consider keeping a daily gratitude journal in which you jot down three things you are grateful for each day. This might be anything from a beautiful sunset to a kind comment from a friend.

DBT is a type of treatment that aims to assist people in regulating their emotions, managing stress, and improving their interpersonal relationships. As previously stated, mindfulness is a basic principle of DBT. Another DBT tenet is distress tolerance, which comprises learning how to deal with unpleasant feelings without resorting to damaging behaviours such as substance abuse or self-harm.

Emotion regulation is another DBT component that comprises learning how to identify and control strong emotions in a healthy way. This ability comprises becoming more aware of one's emotions and learning how to positively respond to them. DBT also emphasises interpersonal effectiveness, or learning how to communicate effectively with others and form meaningful connections.

Finally, creating pleasurable experiences is essential for living a more fulfilling life. Mindfulness, good relationships, and gratitude are all strategies that can help people feel more positive emotions and live happier, more fulfilling lives. DBT concepts can also help persons who suffer with negative thoughts and emotions. By applying these tactics and ideas, individuals can live a life full of joy, meaning, and purpose.

Chapter 10

Maintaining Progress: DBT Techniques and Tools for Continuous Growth and Improvement

My goal as a therapist is to help my clients maintain their gains and continue to grow and improve even after therapy has ended.

Dialectical Behavior Therapy (DBT) is a therapeutic strategy that has been shown to be effective in treating a variety of mental health issues, including mood disorders, anxiety disorders, borderline personality disorder, and substance use disorders.

To maintain development and continue to grow and improve with DBT, it is necessary to use a number of techniques and strategies. One of the most fundamental strategies is mindfulness practice, which comprises paying attention to the present moment without judgement. Mindfulness can help you reduce stress, improve emotional regulation, and generally feel better. Mindfulness can be practised through meditation, yoga, or simply taking a few minutes each day to focus on your breath and notice your thoughts and feelings.

DBT also incorporates skill training, which teaches people specific skills to help them better manage their emotions and actions. These abilities include emotional control, discomfort tolerance, interpersonal effectiveness, and mindfulness. To maintain development and continue to grow and improve, it is vital to continue using these abilities after therapy has stopped. This can be performed by regularly studying the skills, putting them into practice in everyday life, and seeking out more resources to help you extend your understanding and application of the talents.

Another DBT approach for identifying and changing harmful thought patterns is cognitive restructuring. Because unpleasant thoughts can lead to unpleasant feelings and behaviours, learning to recognize and combat these thoughts is critical. To retain progress, grow, and improve, it is vital to continue applying cognitive restructuring techniques after therapy has concluded. This is achieved by regularly checking in with your thoughts and emotions, challenging negative concepts as they arise, and replacing them with more hopeful and realistic views.

Maintaining development and growing and improving demands a strong support system. Included can be family, friends, support groups, and therapists. To retain progress, expand, and improve, it is vital to continue to establish and maintain these support structures. Maintaining touch with friends and family, attending support group meetings, and, if necessary, seeing a therapist can all help.

To summarise, it is tough to maintain progress and continue to grow and improve after therapy, but it is feasible with the right tools and tactics. DBT is a therapy technique that combines mindfulness training, skill development, cognitive restructuring, and support systems. Individuals who use these tools and practices on a regular basis can maintain their progress, grow, and improve their mental health.

Conclusion

As we approach the end of this journey toward emotional well-being and resilience, I'd like to emphasise one final point: change is possible, and it starts with you.

Dialectical Behavior Therapy (DBT) is an effective strategy for building the skills needed to deal with life's challenges with greater ease and confidence. Learning to regulate your emotions, communicate more effectively, and develop healthy relationships can help you live a more happy and meaningful life.

Of course, change is never easy. It takes time, effort, and dedication. However, the rewards are quite worthy of the time and effort. When you commit to personal growth and healing, you open up a world of possibilities for yourself.

Through this book, I've attempted to provide you with the tools and insights you'll need to start your journey toward emotional well-being and resilience. The true effort, however, begins when you put these ideas into reality in your daily life.

Remember that progress is not always linear. Am not assuring you of an easy journey there will be obstacles and challenges. However, if you stay focused on your objectives and keep moving forward, you will eventually achieve greater emotional stability and resilience.

Remember to be kind with yourself as you continue on your journey. Self-compassion and self-care are important, as are acknowledging your accomplishments, no matter how tiny they look. And, if you ever find yourself stuck or overwhelmed, don't be afraid to seek help. There are always resources to assist you on your journey, whether through therapy, support groups, or trusted friends and family.

Finally, let me leave you with this thought: you have the ability to create the life you desire. You are capable of achieving emotional well-being and resilience. And with the right tools, support, and mindset, you can overcome any challenge that comes your way. So take a big breath, believe in yourself, and enjoy the ride.

www.ingramcontent.com/pod-product-compliance
Lightning Source LLC
Chambersburg PA
CBHW051852250726
48659CB00006B/2171